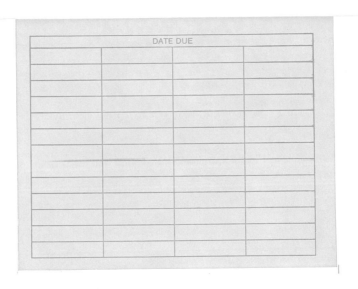

DATE DUE			

NATURE DETECTIVE

Small mammals

ANITA GANERI

Illustrated by John Parsons

FRANKLIN WATTS
NEW YORK • CHICAGO • LONDON • TORONTO • SYDNEY

© 1993 Franklin Watts

Published in the United States
in 1993 by
Franklin Watts, Inc.
95 Madison Avenue
New York, NY 10016

Library of Congress Cataloging-in-Publication Data

Ganeri, Anita, 1961–
    Small mammals / by Anita Ganeri
      p. cm. — (Nature detective)
    Includes index.
    Summary: Discusses the characteristics, habits, and natural habitat of
a variety of small diurnal and nocturnal mammals. Also suggests activities
for observing them and the signs and clues they leave behind.
    ISBN 0-531-14249-3
    1. Mammals—Miscellanea—Juvenile literature. [1. Mammals.]
 I. Title. II. Series: Nature detective (New York, N.Y.)
    QL706.2.G36 1993   92-32706
    599—dc20   CIP AC

Designer: Splash Studio
Editor: Sarah Ridley
Additional illustrations: Terry Pastor

Consultants: Many thanks to
Nigel Hester of the National Trust and
Georgina Wedge of the London Zoo.

Printed in Belgium

Contents

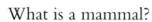

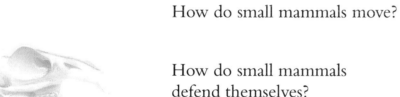

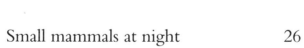

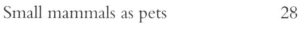

What is a mammal?

The first mammals appeared about 230 million years ago when dinosaurs ruled the earth. They were small, shrewlike creatures that hunted for food at night to avoid the dinosaurs. While the dinosaurs lived, the mammals remained small and hidden away. However, when the dinosaurs died out 65 million years ago, mammals came into their own.

Today there are over 4,500 species of mammals. They range in size from gigantic blue whales to tiny bumblebee bats, and in shape from giraffes to human beings. They are warm-blooded vertebrates (animals with backbones) who have to breathe air to stay alive. They all share certain characteristics, as shown by the red fox (below).

Zoos and wildlife parks are good places to do some detective work on the larger, more unusual mammals. However, with patience, you may be able to observe some small mammals in the wild. Their shape, color, behavior, and habitat will help you to identify them. Even if you do not see the mammals themselves, there are plenty of signs and clues to look for.

Red fox

Ears Mammals are the only animals to have earflaps, and three tiny bones inside each ear. A mammal's earflaps help it to hear better, by channeling sound into its ears. You can use the shape of a mammal's earflaps as a clue to identification.

Mammary glands Mammals are the only animals that feed their young on true milk. It is made in the female's mammary glands, which give the group its name. Most mammals give birth to live young. Many take care of their young for months or even years until they are old enough to fend for themselves.

Teeth The size and shape of mammals' teeth vary according to what they eat. Foxes are carnivores, or meat-eaters. They have long, pointed canine teeth for tearing meat.

Hair Most mammals have some hair on their bodies. It may be in the form of fur, wool, prickles, or spines. Hair helps to insulate the mammal's body against extreme heat or cold. It also traps air to keep the mammal warm. Hair is important for camouflage, too (see page 24).

Backbone Like birds and fish, mammals are vertebrates, or animals with backbones. They have internal skeletons of bone which support their bodies and give them their shape, and also allow them to move.

Tail Some mammals use their tails to help them move and to send messages. Foxes wrap their bushy tails around them to keep warm in winter.

Feet The shape of a mammal's feet varies according to how the mammal moves about. Foxes, like cats and dogs, walk and run on their toes. What looks like a backward-pointing knee is actually a fox's ankle.

The orders of living mammals

Mammals are divided into 21 large groups, called orders. The rodent order is the largest order, containing over 1,700 of the 4,500 known species of mammals. Bats form the second largest order with over 900 species. At the other end of the scale, however, is the aardvark. It is the only member of its order.

Order	Number of species	Examples
Aardvark	1	
Bats	915	Noctule, pipistrelle
Carnivores	231	Fox, weasel
Cetaceans	76	Dolphin, whale
Edentates	36	Anteater, armadillo
Elephants	2	
Elephant shrews	15	
Flying lemurs	2	
Hyraxes	11	
Insectivores	345	Hedgehog, pygmy shrew
Lagomorphs	58	Hare, rabbit
Marsupials	266	Kangaroo
Monotremes	3	Duck-billed platypus
Pangolins	7	
Pinnipedes	33	Seal, sea lion
Primates	181	Bush baby, chimpanzee
Rodents	1,702	Mouse, rat, squirrel
Sirenians	4	Dugong, manatee
Tree shrews	18	
Ungulates (even-toed)	87	Camel, cow, deer
Ungulates (odd-toed)	16	Horse, rhinoceros

Where do mammals live?

Mammals live all over the world, from the baking hot deserts to the icy poles. They are such a successful group of animals because, like birds, they are warm-blooded. This means that they are able to keep a constant body temperature, and therefore remain active, even when their surroundings are very hot or very cold. On the other hand, cold-blooded animals such as reptiles have to rely on the sun to warm them up so that they can function properly. In cold weather, they become very sluggish.

Many small mammals have special features to help them survive in a particular habitat. The way they move, what they eat, and the type of home they have are also linked to where they live. Try to spot these adaptations when you are watching small mammals or reading about them.

Mountain and moorland

Mountain slopes and moorlands are often bleak places where mammals have to cope with biting cold and strong winds. Despite these harsh conditions, many small mammals make their homes in these habitats.

1 Mountain hare In northern climates, the mountain hare changes color according to the seasons. It has a brown coat in summer but turns white in winter. This provides it with year-round camouflage. The hare eats heather and grass.

2 Stoat The stoat also changes color in winter (see page 24) when it is known as ermine. It is mainly nocturnal, hunting for rabbits, rodents, and birds under cover of night. You can tell a stoat apart from its close relative, the weasel, by its larger body and black tail tip.

3 Common shrew The shrew forages among the ground cover for spiders, wood lice, insects, and earthworms. It makes its grass nest under logs or clumps of grass. Listen out for its high, shrill shrieking calls.

4 Common vole

5 Rabbit

City and garden mammals

As their wild homes are destroyed, many small mammals adapt to life in towns and cities. They shelter and look for food in backyards, garbage dumps, and along roadsides.

1 Pipistrelle bat This little bat sometimes nests in the roofs of houses or in the cracks in walls. It hunts at night for insects. Pipistrelles often form very large colonies in summer when they breed, and in winter when they hibernate.

2 House mouse One of the most widely-spread mammals, the house mouse makes its home in houses and farms all over the world. It is very adaptable, making its nest out of anything it can find, including newspaper and scraps of cloth. It eats almost anything, from grain and seeds to clothing.

3 Brown rat Brown rats are found in barns, warehouses, basements, sewers, and garbage dumps. Like house mice, they eat almost anything they can find. They are unwelcome visitors as they cause damage.

4 Red fox

Field and meadow mammals

Many small mammals are attracted to fields and meadows because of the variety of plant food they offer. Sadly, many wild meadows have been cleared to make room for construction and mammals have lost their homes. Farmers, too, try to keep their fields free of mammals that eat their crops.

1 Harvest mouse This tiny mouse uses its tail to help it climb among tall stalks of reeds, grasses, or cereal crops. It weaves its summer nest among tall plants (see page 14) and mainly eats seeds and fruits.

2 Field vole You can tell voles apart from mice by their more rounded heads and short, rounded ears. Field voles make a network of runways among the meadow grass. They follow these to find food. They also dig shallow tunnels just below the surface. These are used for resting and nesting.

3 Mole Moles spend most of their lives underground, so you may not see one unless you are very lucky. However, molehills are a common sight in fields and in gardens. These piles of soil are pushed to the surface by the moles as they dig their tunnels in the earth.

Woodland mammals

Coniferous and deciduous woodlands are good places to look for mammals or for signs of them. Watch for tree branches swaying as squirrels leap across them and for signs of badger sets on the ground.

1 Gray squirrel The gray squirrel is a common sight among oak and beech trees in parks and backyards. Acorns and beechnuts form its staple diet. Its cousins, the rarer red squirrels, prefer coniferous woods.

2 Pine marten A member of the weasel family, the marten is about the size of a small pet cat. It is an excellent climber, often searching for its prey of birds, squirrels, and small rodents among the trees.

3 Noctule bat Large colonies of noctule bats roost in trees, sometimes in holes pecked out by woodpeckers. These large bats fly out at dusk in search of insects to eat.

4 Wood mouse 5 Bank vole

River and pond mammals

Mammals that live near rivers and ponds are often strong swimmers. They swim and dive after their food or to escape from danger. They make their homes on or in the riverbank or pond shore.

1 Otter The otter has a sleek, streamlined shape for cutting through the water. It also has webbed feet to help it swim and waterproof fur to keep it dry. It feeds mainly on fish, especially eels.

2 Water vole The water vole digs its burrow in the riverbank. It swims well to escape from enemies, using a sort of dog paddle. It eats mainly grasses.

3 American mink The American mink is a member of the weasel family. It has dark brown fur and a bushy tail. Mink can grow to two feet in length. They are fierce predators, hunting frogs, fish, and voles.

4 Water shrew 5 Brown rat

Desert mammals

You will probably only be able to see desert mammals in a zoo, but they show very clearly how small mammals adapt to a harsh environment. They have developed ways of coping with the heat and lack of water – the two main problems facing all desert animals.

1 Jerboa Jerboas, kangaroo rats, and gerbils spend the day in underground burrows out of the heat. They plug the burrow entrances with sand to keep them moist and cool. They get food and water from the seeds they eat.

2 Kit fox Desert foxes, such as the kit fox and fennec fox, have huge ears for locating their prey at night and for cooling down. Their ears act like radiators, as the blood running very close to the surface of the ears gives off heat from their bodies.

3 Mojave ground squirrel This small mammal spends days asleep in its underground burrow to avoid long periods of drought. This is the summer equivalent of hibernation. When the squirrel runs, it holds its tail over its back. The white fur on the underside of the tail helps to reflect the sun's heat away from its body.

Mammal watching

Many small mammals are nocturnal or very shy, which makes them difficult to spot. If you go mammal watching, keep downwind (with the wind blowing into your face). Mammals have an acute sense of smell and will disappear as soon as they catch your scent. Wear dull-colored clothes and use the cover of a bush or tree to hide from their sight. Then sit patiently and wait! The best time to look for small mammals is at dawn and dusk, when they are out and about looking for food. Here is some equipment that might help.

Field guide A good field guide is essential for looking up any mammals that you do not recognize.
Notebook and pencils If you see a small mammal, jot down details of its appearance, color, and behavior. Note its special features, such as the size and shape of its ears, and so on. Compare its size to that of a pet cat, dog, or hamster if you have one. Always note the time and date, and the type of habitat you saw the mammal in. Quick sketches of mammals and their tracks are also useful (see page 30).
Binoculars Use binoculars graded 7 x 35 for mammal watching. Choose a light pair that's comfortable to use and easy to carry. They can be expensive, but are worth having.
Plastic bags are good for collecting food remains, such as nibbled nuts or cones, and any hair, fur, or wool you might find snagged on barbed wire fences or on twigs.
Ruler This is useful for measuring mammal tracks. These should be measured lengthwise.

Mammal families

Some small mammals are solitary creatures. They live and hunt by themselves, finding a mate for the breeding season only. Others are very sociable, living together in large colonies. Many mammals live and hunt in a specific area, called a territory. They use scent and droppings to mark its boundaries and to warn off rivals. Some mammals live in a small family group only until their young are able to fend for themselves. It is usually the mother who takes care of them, keeping them from harm, bringing them food, and teaching them to hunt.

All mammals feed their young on milk; they are the only group of animals to do so. Most are known as placental mammals. This means that the baby grows inside its mother's womb and is well developed when it is born. Marsupials, such as wallabies and kangaroos, are mammals with pouches. The babies are born underdeveloped and looking like tiny, hairless, pink grubs. They crawl into their mother's pouch where they suckle on milk and grow. Monotremes are the most unusual mammals. They lay eggs, like reptiles and birds. There are only three species of monotremes – the duck-billed platypus and two species of echidna, or spiny anteater. When the young hatch, however, they suckle on their mother's milk like all other mammal babies.

Brown hares Hares are usually solitary animals. In February and March, however, they gather to mate and breed. To win the attention of a female, rival males take part in spectacular "boxing matches." They kick, chase, and box each other, earning themselves the nickname of "mad March hares."

Brown rat Brown rats groom each other's fur to keep it clean and also to strengthen the bonds between the members of a pack. Like many mammal mothers, rats are quick to protect their young. A mother picks her baby up by the scruff of its neck to carry it away from danger. The baby's automatic reaction is to let its body go limp so that it is easier to carry. This also happens with otters, cats, and dogs.

Bats Some species of bat, including the pipistrelle and noctule bats, are very sociable mammals. They often roost, raise their young, and hibernate in large colonies. In early summer, several hundred female pipistrelles may gather in the roof of a house or barn to breed. This "nursery" is abandoned in August when the young bats fly off. In the winter, both male and female bats congregate in trees and caves to hibernate.

Rabbits Rabbits breed very quickly. A female, or doe, may have twenty babies a year. Each of these is ready to breed when it is about three months old. In Europe and Australia, people have tried to keep the rabbit population down by killing them off with a virus, called myxomatosis. This is carried by fleas. In country areas, ferrets (tamed polecats) are used to hunt and kill rabbits.

Foxes Fox cubs are born in March or April in an underground den, called an earth. The earth is often an old badger set or rabbit burrow. The mother fox suckles her cubs and teaches them how to hunt for food. She shows them how to chase and pounce on rabbits, squirrels, voles, and mice. By the autumn, they are able to fend for themselves. Foxes mark their territory with strong-smelling droppings which they leave on grassy mounds or tree stumps.

Stoats Stoats mate in summer but their babies are not born until the following spring. They are able to slow down the babies' development so that they give birth when conditions are just right for survival. Stoats and weasels may hunt in family groups for a few months, then they split up and lead solitary lives.

Shrews When baby shrews are just two weeks old, their mother takes them with her on hunting trips. If danger threatens, the young shrews line up behind their mother and hang on tightly to the tail of the shrew in front. Then they scurry away, in single file. You can tell baby shrews apart from adults not only by their size but by their hairy tails.

AMAZING FACTS

In the nineteenth century, a prairie dog town in Texas was estimated to contain 400 million animals — enough to cover an area twice the size of Belgium.

Every four years, Norwegian lemmings breed so fast that they run out of space to live. They then seem to panic and rush off to find new land. Many die as they try to cross rivers or the sea.

Nine-banded armadillos give birth to sets of identical quadruplets. Each four are always of the same sex.

The biggest mammal baby is a blue whale calf. It can weigh as much as 2 tons when it is born.

Common voles A female common vole may have her first litter of young when she is just 15 days old. She then produces litters of five to ten babies up to 15 times a year. Common voles live only for one to two years.

Otters Otters hunt for fish in the water, so swimming and diving skills are very important. Otter cubs can swim almost as soon as they are born. But their mother teaches them how to hunt. She brings them a half-dead fish which they practice chasing and catching. This play-hunting also strengthens the bond between the mother and her cubs.

Prairie dogs about town

Prairie dogs, or ground squirrels, live on the plains and prairies of the western United States. They live together in huge systems of burrows, called "towns." Several thousand animals may live in one town. Each town is divided up into smaller neighborhoods, called "wards." In turn, these are split into smaller, family units, called "coteries." A coterie is home to a male, up to four females, and any of their young that are under two years of age.

When two prairie dogs meet, they "kiss" by rubbing their noses and incisor teeth together. This allows them to identify if the other animal is a friend or enemy. Sentries keep guard over the burrows. If they spot danger, they bark to sound the alarm and send the other prairie dogs diving into their burrows for safety.

Mammals at home

Most small mammals need a home of some type to provide a safe place to rest and raise their young, as well as shelter from harsh weather or hungry enemies. Homes include nests, burrows, holes and hollows, and scrapes in the ground. Some mammals make temporary homes which are used for breeding, then abandoned. Others, such as badgers, use the same home for several generations. Some small mammals, such as harvest mice and beavers, are superb builders. Others, such as bats, do not build but use hollow trees or caves as roosts. Rats and mice will make their nests almost anywhere – in sewers, under floorboards, and in cracks in walls. Many small mammal homes have special names, such as a fox's earth, a badger's set, a squirrel's drey, and an otter's holt.

Animals make their homes out of a variety of materials including grass, leaves, bark, sheep's wool, feathers, fur, and even newspapers.

Homes above ground

Some small mammals make their homes on the ground itself, up on tree branches, inside tree trunks, or on tall plants.

Harvest mouse A harvest mouse weaves its summer breeding nest from grass, leaves, or stalks of corn. It shreds the plant leaves with its teeth but does not detach them from the stem. This wedges the nest firmly on the plant stalk above the ground. Then it lines the nest with soft grass, feathers, or wool. The nests are about the size of baseballs and may be home to as many as eight babies and their mother. In winter, harvest mice nest among tree roots or in underground burrows.

Hare Hares do not dig burrows, as rabbits do. Instead, they hollow out a hiding place among the grass, soil, or even snow. This is called a form. A hare rests in its form during the day and its young, called leverets, are born in the form. Unlike baby rabbits, newborn leverets are covered in fur and their eyes are already open, so they do not need the protection of an underground burrow as rabbits do.

Squirrel Squirrels build their nests, or dreys, out of twigs, bark, and grass. They line them with any soft material they can find, including feathers and sheep's wool, and even newspaper in cities. The dreys are about the size of soccer balls. Squirrels build sturdier dreys for winter and flimsier ones for summer. Look out for dreys wedged into forks in trees. They will be easier to see in winter when the trees are bare of leaves. Never disturb the drey – a squirrel may be asleep inside.

Underground homes

Underground burrows provide small mammals with safety and shelter. Most small mammals have to leave their burrows to feed, although moles spend most of their lives underground.

Rabbit Rabbits dig out huge underground networks of burrows, called warrens. The entrance and exit holes are easy to spot above ground and are often marked by dark brown, pea-sized droppings. Inside a warren, there are burrows for resting and breeding. The breeding burrows are called stops. The young rabbits are born here in nests of fur and grass. They are blind, furless, and helpless at birth.

Mole Molehills are the only obvious sign of a mole's underground tunnel system. The largest molehill is called the fortress. It stands over the mole's main nest or its food store. Moles dig through the soil with their spade-like front paws. They are champion diggers, excavating tunnels over 330 feet long. They usually live alone.

Water vole Water voles make their nests in burrows in the riverbank or on the pond or lake shore. There are several entrances to the burrows, both above and below the surface of the water. Inside there is a nesting chamber and sometimes a store of plant food for winter.

Master builders

Badgers Badgers live in trees, hollow logs, and deep burrows, often among the roots of trees. There are entrance holes and ventilation holes on the surface and, inside, there are chambers for sleeping and breeding. Badgers are very houseproud animals. They replace dirty bedding regularly and spring clean the set once a year. Look for dropped fern, hay, and leaves near the entrance to a set. They use special pits dug outside the set as toilets. Badgers live in family groups, or clans, of up to 12 animals.

Beavers Beavers are the master engineers of the mammal world. They build homes, called lodges. First, they fell trees and cut them into logs using their incredibly strong incisor teeth. Then, they dam a slow-moving river or stream with the logs, some boulders, and mud. In the pond formed by the dam, they build their dome-shaped lodge of wood. Inside the lodge is a living chamber. The only way into it is through an underwater tunnel.

The longest beaver dam known was 2,300 feet long and strong enough to bear the weight of a person on horseback. Next to the lodge, on the pond bottom, beavers keep a supply of young trees. These provide them with bark to eat in the harsh winter.

Winter sleep

Some small mammals, such as hedgehogs, dormice, and bats, hibernate in the winter to avoid the cold weather and lack of food. They stock up on food in autumn to build up their fat supplies, then live off these as they sleep. To save their energy, their breathing and pulse rates slow down and their body temperature drops. They remain barely alive until the warm spring weather comes. Marmots hibernate for the longest time. They may spend nine months of the year asleep.

Other small mammals, such as foxes and squirrels, spend days sleeping and sheltering in their warm dens. But they do not hibernate. They have to come out of their dens to hunt for food.

Dormouse The name dormouse means "sleeping mouse." This mammal hibernates from October to April in a nest in a hollow tree or even in an empty bird nesting box in the backyard. Dormice become very fat before they hibernate, by eating large amounts of nuts and seeds.

Hedgehog Hedgehogs hibernate from October to April in a nest of dry leaves on the ground. The nest may be hidden among bushes or in the corner of a garden shed.

Bat Bats hibernate in caves, hollow trees, and buildings. They hang upside down with their wings wrapped around their bodies. You should never pick up a hibernating bat. It will waste precious energy waking up and may die.

Bats are hardy hibernators. The red bat of North America can hibernate in very low temperatures and can even survive when parts of its body freeze solid.

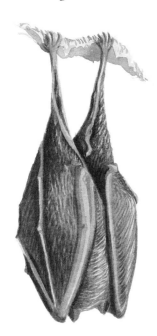

Anyone at home?

Even if you do not catch sight of the mammal itself, you may find clues leading you to its home. Molehills are easy to find, but keep a look out, too, for piles of earth which may show the position of a fox's earth or a badger's set. You may smell a fox's musty scent around its earth. Watch for dropped bedding or nest materials and for tracks, hair or fur, droppings, and patches of flattened vegetation. Never damage or remove homes you find. They may be in use or waiting to be reused.

What do small mammals eat?

A mammal's diet depends on where the mammal lives and whether it is better adapted to eating plants or hunting and catching other animals. Animals that eat plants are called herbivores; meat-eaters are called carnivores. Most small mammals are omnivores – they eat a mixture of plants and meat. Even foxes, which are carnivores, will eat fruit and berries if their rabbit or rodent prey is scarce. Whatever their diet, small mammals spend a large part of their lives searching for enough to eat. Food provides them with the energy they need to keep their body temperature constant and to remain active.

Mammal diets

Here you can see some examples of what small mammals eat and how they collect or catch their food.

Squirrel Like many rodents, squirrels hide nuts and seeds away for winter, when food is scarce. They often forget where they have hidden them. Their food stores, or caches, are often found inside hollow tree trunks. Squirrels eat nuts, such as acorns and beechnuts, and cones. They hold them in their front paws and gnaw away at them to get to the kernels or seeds inside. They will also eat spring buds and bark.

Mice House mice will eat almost anything, though their main diet is grain and seeds. In people's houses, they will gnaw their way through paper, cheese, string, electric cables, and even frozen meat. Wood mice mainly eat seeds but will also catch insects, worms, and snails. They often store food underground, or in old birds' nests or nesting boxes.

Mole Moles hunt for their food of earthworms underground, sniffing them out with their long, sensitive snouts. Because it does not need its eyes to see underground, a mole's eyes are tiny and weak. Moles do not eat all the worms they catch at once. They bite the heads off some and store them underground for later. A mole can eat its own weight in worms a day.

Weasel Weasels have very slim bodies, and are only the size of small rats. They have no problem following mice and voles into their underground burrows and pouncing on them. They bite their prey on the back of the neck to kill it. Weasels also climb trees to catch birds and steal their eggs.

Otter Otters mainly eat fish that they catch in the water. They bring their catch to the shore and eat it on land, holding it in their front paws. They have sharp canine teeth for tearing the fish apart. Otters eat eels, trout, sticklebacks, and other fish. They also catch shellfish, water voles, frogs, and birds.

Common shrew Shrews are very small mammals but they have huge appetites. They have to eat their own weight in food every day to stay alive. So they spend most of their lives foraging for insects, slugs, spiders, worms, and some plant food to eat. Shrews belong to the order of insectivores – the insect-eating mammals.

AMAZING FACTS

Mole rats, a type of rodent, use their front teeth to dig their underground tunnel systems.

A great vampire bat laps up about two teaspoonsful of blood a day. It attacks horses and cattle while they are asleep at night.

Pikas are small mammals that look similar to guinea pigs. In summer, they gather plant stems and make them into haystack-like piles. This supply of food lasts them throughout the winter when food is scarce.

Pond bat Most bats are insect–eaters, catching moths and flies at dusk. Pond bats swoop low over the water, sometimes picking insects off the surface. In the tropics, there are also bats that eat fruit, fish, and frogs, and, of course, vampire bats who live on animal blood.

Red fox In some cities, red foxes scavenge for scraps of food in garbage cans and garbage dumps. They often hide or bury excess food, returning for it later. They are carnivores, eating rabbits, birds, and rodents. They also eat birds' eggs, insects, fruit such as apples, and berries. Henhouses are sometimes raided by foxes at night.

Gnawers, gnashers, and grinders

A mammal's teeth are a good clue to its diet. Rodents, such as mice and squirrels, have long, chisel-like front teeth called incisors. These help them to gnaw food. The incisors continue to grow throughout a rodent's life, but they are constantly being worn down by gnawing. Carnivores, such as weasels, have special piercing teeth called canines for tearing at meat. Insect-eaters, such as bats and shrews, have small, sharp teeth and fanglike canines for chewing their insect food. Rabbits and hares have two pairs of incisors, together with flat, blunt cheek teeth for chewing plants and grass.

Rabbit   **Cat**   **Hedgehog**

Squirrel

Hamster

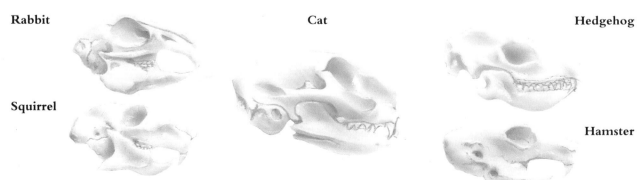

Looking at leftovers

Many mammals leave signs that they have been feeding nearby. Look for nibbled nuts, seeds, fruit, bones, and any teeth marks on them. Then try to identify the type of mammal that has left them – you should be able to find this out in your field guide. Here are some of the clues you might find.

Holes in nuts such as hazelnuts or acorns are often the work of rodents, such as mice or squirrels. Wood mice and dormice gnaw round holes in nuts; squirrels sometimes split them in half.

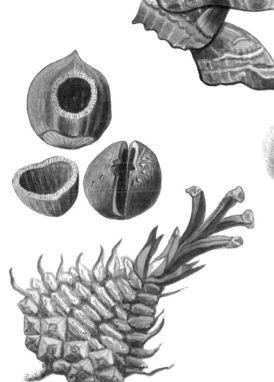

Piles of moth or other insect wings under a tree may be the leftovers of a bat colony's meal. The bats eat the insects' juicy bodies but discard their wings.

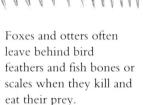

If you find teeth marks on tree bark in winter, they may have been made by voles, hares, or rabbits. In spring, squirrels strip bark off the upper part of the trunk to get at the sap underneath.

Foxes and otters often leave behind bird feathers and fish bones or scales when they kill and eat their prey.

Gnawed pinecones are often left behind by squirrels. They bite the scales off to reach the seeds hidden inside. Some birds eat and discard cones too, but they do not usually peck the scales off.

Laying bait

Many small mammals come out to look for food at dawn and dusk. You can encourage them to appear by leaving out food for them. Make sure that there are no cats about. Peanuts, raisins, rolled oats, acorns, and seeds are tempting bait for rodents. You could also try cabbage, carrots, and lettuce for rabbits. Badgers are very fond of the taste of honey. For weasels and stoats, place the bait in a short piece of pipe to make them feel at home. Minced meat makes good bait for these small carnivores.

How do small mammals move?

Small mammals often need to move very quickly to escape from danger and to find food. They move in a variety of ways – running, swimming, climbing, flying, hopping, and burrowing. Many of them have special features to help them move. These include long legs, webbed feet, wings, claws, and long tails. A small mammal's general shape and these features in particular are good clues to how it moves.

Balancing act Rats, mice, and squirrels use their long tails for balance as they run and jump. Harvest mice coil their tails around corn and grass stems to support them as they climb. Squirrels are very agile climbers. They leap from branch to branch, and often run down trees headfirst.

Digging and burrowing Moles use their large, strong front feet as spades for digging through the soil. They are able to move smoothly through their tunnels because their fur can lie in any direction and does not catch on the tunnel walls. Badgers dig with the claws on their front feet. They have stocky, wedge-shaped bodies for pushing through the ground.

Leaping and hopping Rabbits and hares have very long back legs which help them to hop at high speed. At top speed, a hare can reach an amazing 50 mph. When rabbits and hares hop fast, their longer back feet come in front of their shorter front feet. The soles of their feet are hairy to give them a better grip on the ground and to cushion them.

Swimming Otters are superbly adapted for swimming. They have webbed feet and rudderlike tails to propel them through the water. They can close their nostrils and ears underwater. Their bodies are sleek and streamlined for cutting through the water. Mink are also good swimmers, although their feet are only partly webbed.

Tracking and trailing

You may find mammal tracks and footprints in the soft mud around rivers, ponds, and puddles or in freshly fallen snow. You could also try putting down a layer or tray of slightly damp sand in your backyard. Leave it overnight and see if any small mammals have walked over it by morning. You can look up any tracks you find in your field guide. Measure the tracks from heel to toe. Make a note of how many toes there are in each footprint and if there are any claw marks. Hare and rabbit tracks look similar, but hare tracks are bigger and farther apart. You can find out more about recording tracks on page 31.

Flying mammals

Bats are the only mammals that can fly. Their wings have evolved from their hands. This gives the bat order its scientific name of *Chiroptera*, or "handwings." A bat's wing is made of skin stretched between its very long second and fifth finger bones. Its thumb is left free for grooming and gripping. The wings are also attached to the bat's back legs and sometimes to its tail. A bat flaps its wings as it flies, as a bird does.

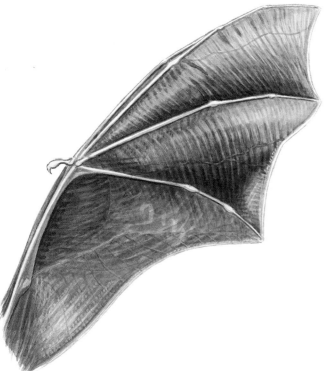

AMAZING FACTS

The fastest land mammal over a short distance is the cheetah. It can bound along at over 60 mph after its prey. It has an incredibly flexible backbone which allows it to move so fast.

North American porcupines are good at climbing trees. They have fleshy, no-skid pads on their feet to give them grip.

The fastest-flying bat known is a Brazilian free-tailed bat. It was timed at 30 mph.

Sloths are the slowest land mammals. Their top speed on the ground is about 5 feet per minute. Up in the trees they speed up to about 15 feet per minute.

How do small mammals defend themselves?

Small mammals have many enemies, including larger mammals, birds of prey, and people. They have different ways of defending themselves. Some simply run, hop, swim, or fly away. Others use color to warn their enemies or camouflage to hide themselves from sight. Some small mammals have special weapons to protect themselves, such as sharp claws, spiky coats, and terrible smells. Many of these features are useful clues to identification.

Thumping a warning When rabbits leave their warren to feed, they are constantly alert to danger. If an enemy is spotted, one of the rabbits thumps its back feet on the ground to warn the others. They then dive down the nearest bolt hole into the safety of the warren.

Color and camouflage Stoats and mountain hares change color to match their surroundings. In summer, they are brown to blend in with the mountain slopes or moorland where they live. In winter, their coats turn white so that they are camouflaged against the snow and ice. The only part of a stoat that does not turn white is the black tip of its tail. A mountain hare turns white except for the tips of its ears.

Freezing solid If a hare senses danger, it "freezes," or crouches completely still. It then runs away if the danger gets closer. Field voles may also freeze if they are out hunting and a bird of prey flies overhead.

Smelly skunks Skunks live in North and South America, so you may only be able to see them in a zoo. They have two methods of self-defense. Their striking black and white coats act as a warning sign to enemies. If this does not work, the skunk turns its back, stamps its feet, and raises its tail. Then it squirts out a stream of foul-smelling liquid at its enemy. The liquid can burn the skin, and the smell takes days to disappear.

Poisonous bite Only two types of mammal are poisonous. One is the water shrew which has poisonous saliva. When it bites into its prey of fish, frogs, and other small mammals, the saliva paralyzes the prey. The water shrew also secretes a foul-tasting liquid from glands on its skin which makes it unappetising to predators. Male duck-billed platypuses are the only other poisonous mammals. They have poisonous spurs on their back legs.

A whiff of polecat
Polecats live mainly in woodland but they are also found around farms and rivers. They have special glands under their tails which make a very strong-smelling musk. When a polecat is threatened or frightened, it releases a burst of musk to warn its enemy off.

Spikes and spines

European hedgehog A hedgehog's main form of defense is its spiky coat. An adult hedgehog may have up to 7,000 sharp spines, each ¾ to 1 inch long. The spines have developed from hairs. When danger threatens, a hedgehog curls itself up into a tight ball. Very few predators are willing to risk tackling such a prickly mouthful.

North American porcupine Porcupines are covered in thousands of long, sharp quills which are excellent protection. Like a hedgehog's spines, these have grown from hairs. When a porcupine is attacked, it runs into its attacker or lashes out with its tail. The quills detach when they are embedded in the attacker's skin, where they can cause fatal wounds if infection sets in.

Small mammals at night

Many small mammals are nocturnal. They come out at night to hunt for food. During the day they hide and rest in burrows, dens, and roosts. There are several advantages to a nocturnal life-style. The mammals are not competing for food with daytime animals and do not run the risk of attack by daytime enemies. There are, however, some dangerous nocturnal hunters, such as foxes and birds of prey.

Nocturnal mammals have special features that help them to find their way and find food in the dark. These include very acute eyesight, hearing, and sense of smell.

Sense of smell Mammals that hunt in the dark, such as moles and badgers, have poor eyesight. They find their food by using their superb hearing and sense of smell. Badgers and foxes usually hunt along well-used tracks, which they have marked with their own particular smell.

Eyes and ears Wood mice spend the day hidden among tree roots or in a tunnel underground. They come out at night to forage for nuts, seeds, and berries. They have large ears and eyes to help them in the dark, and to keep a lookout for danger. Wood mice are the staple diet of many owls, foxes, and weasels.

Camouflage Badgers and raccoons have striking black and white coats. Instead of making them stand out, however, they help to hide the animals at night. The black and white pattern breaks up the outline of the mammal's body, making it very difficult to see in the fading light.

Daytime den The pine marten spends the day resting in a hole in a hollow tree trunk or between some rocks. It hunts alone at dusk and dawn for rodents, birds and their eggs, and squirrels. It also eats honey and berries.

Bats on the wing

Bats use sound to "see" at night as they fly in search of insects. This is called echolocation. As they fly, they make very high-pitched squeaking sounds, too high for us to hear. These sounds hit any objects in the bat's path, whether it be a moth or a tree, and send back echoes. The bat picks up the returning echoes with its large, extremely sensitive ears. From them, it can tell what lies ahead and fly away from an obstacle or toward a meal.

Watch out for bats as they leave their roosts at dusk. Look for their silhouettes in the sky. Note the size and shape of their wings and the pattern they make as they fly. This will help you to identify them.

Watching mammals at night

The best way to watch nocturnal mammals is to use a flashlight with a piece of red cellophane taped over its beam. Small mammals with eyes adapted for seeing at night cannot see red light very well so it does not disturb them. You need to take up your watching position well before dusk when the mammals emerge. You could use bait to lure them out (see page 21).

Horseshoe bat This bat gets its name from the shape of the fleshy "nose leaves" on its nose. It uses them for squeaking when its mouth is full of food. Horseshoe bats fly low after insects, flapping their wings slowly like giant butterflies.

Noctule bat The noctule bat is one of the first to appear on a warm evening. It often hunts at the same time as swallows and swifts. It sometimes flies in a group, swooping and diving after insects.

Long-eared bat As its name suggests, the long-eared bat has very long ears, almost as long as its body. The bases of its ears meet on the top of its head. This bat has a slow, fluttering flight and can hover by trees to snap insects off the leaves.

Common pipistrelle Pipistrelles are found around farms and houses. They fly quickly and jerkily after insects. They are the smallest of the European bats.

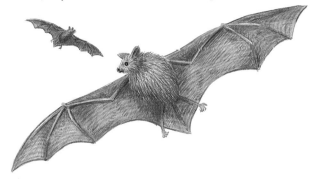

Small mammals as pets

Many people keep small mammals, such as gerbils, guinea pigs, mice, rats, and rabbits, as pets. This is certainly an excellent way of observing small mammals closely. You must, however, be prepared to work hard taking care of your pet. It relies on its owner to feed it and keep its cage clean. Most pets have been bred from wild ancestors. You should not try to keep unusual pets, such as monkeys or snakes. It is too difficult to reproduce the living conditions they are used to in the wild.

Guinea pig Guinea pigs are related to South American rodents, such as cavies, agoutis, and porcupines. They have the chisellike incisor teeth typical of rodents. You may need to get a veterinarian to file these down if they do not get enough wear. Buy or make your guinea pig a hutch large enough to have a separate sleeping area. You could also make it a run outside so that it gets enough exercise. Guinea pigs eat oats, seeds, grass, and vegetables.

Mice and rats Mice and rats are intelligent, inquisitive animals that make good pets. Never keep mice and rats together, however. The white mice and rats that people keep as pets are descended from wild ancestors. They do not spread diseases like their wild cousins but you should clean their cages out regularly as they can become smelly. Mice and rats are very active, agile mammals. Make sure they have a wheel, ladders, or a piece of tubing to play on.

Keeping a pet diary

A good way of studying your pet is to keep a diary about it. See how fast it grows, by measuring and weighing it every three days while it is young. Note down how many hours a day it spends asleep, feeding, grooming, and exercising. Does it do each thing at the same time every day, or do the times vary? Does it have a favorite food? Does it like being stroked? You should soon build up a good picture of your pet's behavior and life-style.

Rabbits Keep pet rabbits in a hutch outside. Bring them in if the weather gets very cold. Take them out regularly to stroke and groom them, and give them a run. Rabbits are very clean animals. Remove any dirty bedding or old food from their hutch every day and clean it thoroughly once a week.

Hamsters Hamsters need strong cages so that they do not gnaw their way out. They are most active in the late evening, sleeping for most of the day. It is best to feed them in the evening just after they wake up. Watch your hamster as it eats, stuffing its cheek pouches with seeds, then pushing them out and hiding them in the corners of its cage.

AMAZING FACTS

It is thought that all the pet hamsters in the world are descended from one wild female ancestor. She was found in Syria in 1930 with a litter of 30 young.

Record pet litters include 34 babies to a house mouse, 26 babies to a golden hamster, and 24 to a white rabbit.

A tortoiseshell cat, called Towser, was the greatest mouser ever. In her lifetime she caught some 28,900 mice, at the rate of about three per day.

There are about 6.5 million pet cats in Britain and about 54.5 million in the United States.

The smallest dog on record was a Yorkshire terrier. It was only the size of a matchbox.

The largest pet dogs are old English mastiffs and St. Bernards. The tallest are great danes and Irish wolfhounds. They can stand over 3 feet tall at the shoulder.

More things to do

Sketching small mammals

If you do catch a glimpse of a small mammal, a quick sketch is a good way of remembering what it looks like so you can identify it later in your field guide. Your drawing doesn't have to be a masterpiece. You could practice by drawing a sleeping pet dog or cat, if you have one. Use simple shapes, such as circles, rectangles, and lines to show the basic outline of the mammal's body. Label any features you notice, such as the mammal's length, height, and any patches of different colors on its fur. Don't forget to note down when and where you saw the mammal and what it was doing.

Making a hide

It is essential to be still and keep out of sight when you are watching small mammals. They will pick up the vibrations of even your softest footsteps and run away. You can use the cover of bushes or trees to hide yourself. Crouch down to prevent your body outline or silhouette from being seen. You could make a simple hide out of bamboo canes, leaves and twigs, and brown or green colored material. Tie the bamboo canes firmly at the top to make a wigwamlike frame. It should be big enough for you to sit in. Then cover the frame with the fabric, leaves, and twigs to make it look as natural as possible. You will need to cut slits in the material as viewing windows.

Making a bat box

You can attract bats to your garden by building them a nesting or roosting box. You will need six pieces of wood, each 4 inches by 4 inches.

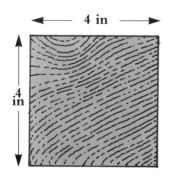

← **4 in** →

4 in

1 Cut about 1 inch off the end of one piece. This will form the entrance to the box.

2 Nail the wood together as shown below, with the entrance on the underside. Then nail it to a larger piece of wood and attach it to a tree or fence. It should be about 7 feet above the ground.

Keeping track

You can make plaster casts of any mammal footprints or tracks you find. The best place to look for them is in wet mud around ponds or in parks after rain.

1 Make a cardboard collar from a piece of cardboard about 12 inches long and 3 inches high. Staple the ends together.

2 Place the collar around the prints. Then mix up some plaster of Paris in an old measuring cup and pour it into the collar so that it reaches about halfway up the cardboard. Let the plaster of Paris set, according to the package's instructions.

3 Then remove the collar and lift the cast up gently. Wash the cast in cold water. Which mammal do you think made the tracks? Was it walking or running at the time?

Droppings detection

Many small mammals, such as rabbits, foxes, and badgers, leave their droppings in set places away from their homes. These are a good sign that there are small mammals nearby, as well as providing clues as to what the mammals have eaten. Droppings

A small mammal scrapbook

Keep a scrapbook record of any small mammals you see in the wild or in a zoo or wildlife park. Use a strong scrapbook or loose-leaf ring binder. Write your field notes in it and stick in any sketches, photos, or postcards of the animals. You could divide your scrapbook into sections relating to the different groups of small mammals, such as rodents, insectivores, carnivores, and so on. The chart of mammal orders on page 5 will help you.

Another idea for your scrapbook is to make a mammal map of your neighborhood. Draw a simple map of the area around your house, including any woodland, wasteland, streams, ponds, and fields. Mark on it any mammals or signs of mammals that you see, including fur, droppings, leftover food, and tracks.

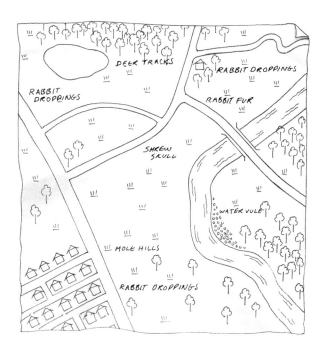

from herbivores (plant-eaters), such as rabbits, tend to be smaller and rounder. Droppings from carnivores (meat-eaters), such as foxes and otters, tend to be longer and more irregular in shape. They often contain bones, fish scales, hair, and feathers.

Index